Manage Stress Anxiety and improve your Mental Focus (Tips & Hints)

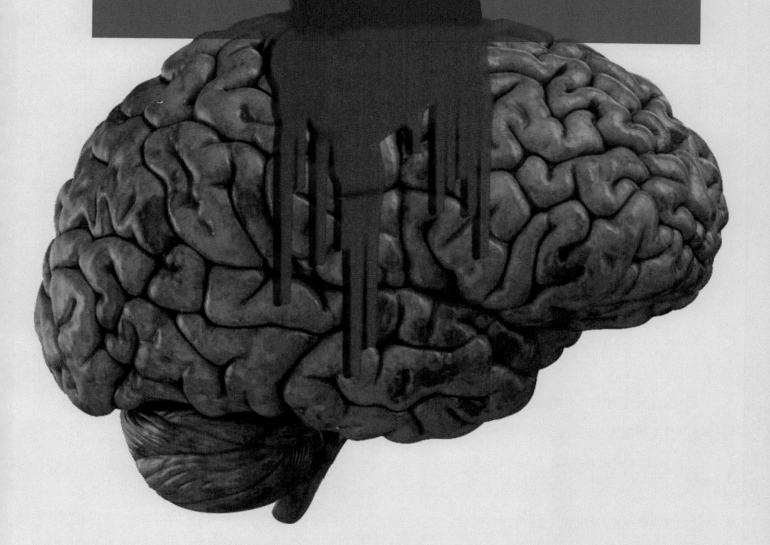

Dr Patrice Mbowa Kasongo

Table Of Contents

About the Author

Patrice Mbowa Kasongo is an animal lovers' and Veterinarian by profession living in United Kingdom who likes sharing knowledge and helping others on the topic of science.

My first research publications was entitled "How stressors affect pigs health" in 1988. Among scientific works published,
I produced in 2002 another piece of work entitled " How to improve goat productivity by genes manipulation" This research publications was done to win my Masters' Degree in Science from Liege University (Belgium).

In the United Kingdom I have benefited from further studies with University of Edinburgh and Cambridge Expert VETS at Madingley Hall at University of Cambridge in 2008 and 2009,

In 2015 I published another research on Hamster's behaviour with Taylor Hill Centre part of Kirklees College in Huddersfield,

Patrice's words of wisdom **"Life is all about keeping your smile alive"**

Everyone deserve to be happy and feeling that they're improving, no matter what stage in life they're in, whether it's to develop a better mindset or good health.

Progress is the Key.

INTRODUCTION

There is probably nothing more crushing then looking at the sky knowing that the future of humanity is at stake; businesses are closing downs, people are losing their jobs, relationships are broken apart and a lot more... With this unprecedent time we are living in, not knowing what the future hold for us.

Time and time again , if we study history, we will realise that every crisis has been the trigger, the turning point for creativity, growth ,new leadership; as a result of that human being should have to adapt to new way of survival, new way of doing business and more importantly the opportunity of the human race to shift its mindset and engage radically in the new pathway of the champion.

This eBook is meant to inspire you, to educate you, to give you capabilities and wake you up at your inner strength for you to challenge adversity.

Why do we need to adjust our body? mind?

We do know that health is the wonderful gift the universe, the creator has given to us, we have the duty to maintain it; in other words doing what it takes to build a stronger immune system that put us in the first line of life competition.

The 4 winning punches of healthy life

This book laid out the concept in a very specific way,

4 sections, all grounded in the late knowledge in science and based of life experiences.

Section 1: **Stress**

Section 2: **Mind**

Section 3: **Dietary intake**

Section 4: **Sleep and Exercises**

By the end of this eBook, you will gain an understanding of what the stress is and how to deal with it, you will also assimilate how to adjust your mind to combat depression, anxiety, fear, unhealthy thoughts , you will then digest what to eat to get the nutrients needed to fight viral infection and in the end you will know inside out all aspects to better sleep and exercises.

I can assure you that you'll master the necessary knowledge needed to get your body defence mechanism stronger and your mental health under control; the bottom line being able to get the necessary tools that will equip you to stand up, rise up in this unprecedent crisis due to "*virus war*" supported by a strong immune system.

The following pages will dive deeper in understanding and overcoming obstacles to a healthy and joyful life.

The 4 Winning- Punches of healthy life.

Chap 1 : Stress management

1.1 What is Stress?

This concept is commonly use in our daily life when we feel emotional hold down by situation, we are in. When someone say I feel stressed, I am stressed.

What does it mean by that?

Events that put pressure on us – for instance, times where we have lots to do and think about or do not have much control over what is happening.

The way we react because of being put under pressure – the feelings we get when we face the situation and we find difficult to cope with.

In fact, "Stress" is the body's reaction to feeling threatened or under pressure.

1.2 Expert advice

When you are experiencing stress, the first step is identifying what the exact source of that stresses.

Sometimes this is easy, and we can identify exactly what is causing us to feel this way.

Sometimes, it is trickier taking control of the situation when you are feeling stressed is really empowering and it can help you find a solution to the way you feel.

Think ahead can really help you when you are feeling stressed because it helps you take control of the situation. it means that if you have got a stressful day or a stressful week coming up, if you can think ahead you will feel more able to cope with it.

So this might be simple things like just preparing the evening before so that you are not in a mad rush the next day or trying to think about ways you can schedule breaks in your day or during your week to do something that you enjoy that will make you feel better and more able to cope.

Having a regular routine, which you will find useful for you to kind of feel you in control of things that really, really helps.

Physical activity is one of the best things you can do to try and help you deal with stress. We will take you out of the situation and it will help you lay ahead and make you calmer and more able to deal with the situation when you are back in it.

The 4 winning punches of healthy life

One of the tools you can use to deal with stress is to challenge yourself. This can be in work or outside of work, taking up new goals, new challenges, maybe new hobbies. This can be very empowering, and it can help build your confidence when you are learning new things that can help build emotional resilience.

This will help you deal with stress in those things I do, both in terms of general lifestyle, but also specific things in terms of stress, anxiety to reduce them and also doing some coaching with children I find useful and indoors during a really good thing to reduce stress.

You will also find physical exercise a big part for you in reducing stress, just having a sense of kind of wellbeing and being healthy.

Yoga and exercise are great for men or a woman for anybody. They are good events.

Swimming is nice, walk in a park, admire things in the wood.

Positive thinking is an important way of dealing with some of the signs of stress when you particularly feeling stressed.

It can be a time where it is very difficult to actually look at the positive, but it is very important to try and look at some of the things you might be grateful for and some of the positive things that have happened each day.

Some people find it useful at the end of the day to write down three things that were positive that happened that day, or that they are grateful for something that you'll find beneficial when you are dealing with stress is to avoid some of the more unhealthy behaviours that sometimes we use to help us try and cope stress like drinking alcohol or smoking or drinking a lot of caffeine.

These are things that might make us feel better in the short term, but in the longer term, we are just going to lead to more problems. In fact, giving up smoking can be a positive way to help you feel better.

Sometimes dealing with stress can feel like you are dealing with a massive problem and it can make you put off even starting to try and handle the situation.

One of the best, most helpful things you can do is to try and break it down into manageable chunks and then just work through those chunks one at a time and give yourself credit when you get to each part because you are getting there towards the final goal.

The 4 winning punches of healthy life

Some stressful situations are out of our control, and it is at times like that we need to try and focus on the elements that we can control. So while there may be a bigger problem, there may be some things, some actions you can take, things that you can do that are under your control that will help you feel more confident.

Helping other people can really help you build up your own emotional strengths and improve your wellbeing; this might be helping people through volunteer work or it might just be helping your family or helping a neighbour with small tasks that they are unable to do, such as the shopping.

The more you learn about yourself, the more you learn how to cope the world and techniques and things that you need to consider. It is going to be easier for you to manage your life.

1.3 What happens to our bodies when we are stressed?

Before we go further, let us have a look at human anatomy about this study.

1.3.1 Parts of body involved in the stress

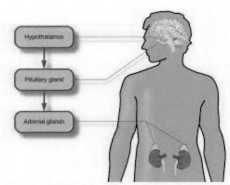

On this chart, let us have a look at the major organs involved in the stress.

1.3.1.1 Brain

we do have what is called the limbic system referred as the centre of emotions, which is a group of interconnected structures located deep within the brain.

It is the part of brain that is responsible for behavioural and emotional responses, Fear, anger, anxiety, depression, happiness, love and so on.

The structures that make up the:

limbic system

-*Hypothalamus*: involved in controlling emotion, sexual response, hormones release and regulation of the body temperature.

-*Hippocampus*: Helps preserve and retrieve memories and is also involved in the understanding the spatial dimension of the environment you are in.

-*Amygdala*: play a major role in fear and anger and helps also coordinate responses to things in your environment, those that especially trigger an emotional response

-*Limbic cortex*: made up of two structures,

- Cingulate gyrus
- The para hippocampal gyrus

Impact mood, motivation, and judgement.

1.3.1.2 Pituitary gland or Hypophysis

A small pea-sized gland that plays a major role in regulating vital body function and general wellbeing, it is referred to as the body's master gland in that it controls the activity of most other hormone-secreting glands.

1.3.1.3 Adrenal gland

located on top of each kidney as shown above. They are endocrine gland meaning that they pour in the blood stream chemical called hormones.

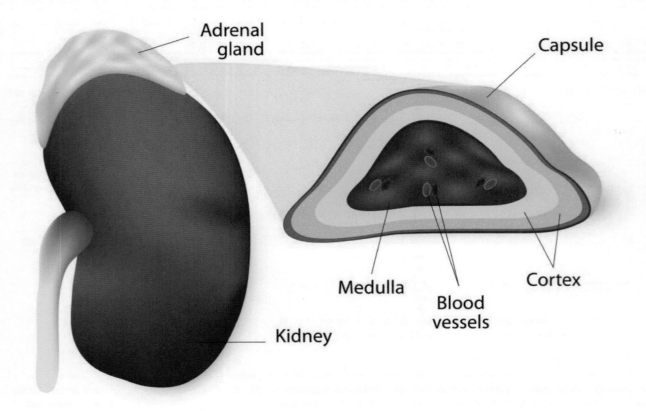

Adrenal gland has 2 part to it,

The adreno cortex that is the outer section

The adreno medulla that is the inner section

The outer part is a true gland as it secretes hormones called glucocorticoid (cortisol) involved in the stress process.

Cortisol

-Suppress inflammation when there is injury

-Raise sugar in the blood by promoting the breakdown of proteins into sugar and turning sugar into fat. (at high level in the bloodstream)

-Suppress the immune response leaving the person vulnerable to get sick (at high level in the bloodstream)

The inner part, has a nervous connection from the brain down to the adreno medulla to secrete adrenalin that is responsible of all obvious change in the body following a stress situation:

Adrenalin

-Increase metabolism

-Trigger the fight and flight response

-Raise alertness

-Suppress the digestive functions

In the body information is processed and conveyed through two pathways Nervous system and the endocrine system

When flies land on your skin, information is transmitted from the sensitive nerves to the brain and the brain give a quick signal to the hand muscle to react, what we see here, is that the information is sent quickly to a clear destination or target a specific cell.

but the endocrine system act though the release of chemical called hormone produced in the organ named gland.

Hormones are sent through the blood stream and diffuse in the body.

Glossary:

CRH: Corticotrophin-releasing hormone is the main element that drives the body's response to stress produce by hypothalamus neuron

ACTH: Adrenocorticotropic hormone (ACTH) is made in the pituitary gland. It is needed for your adrenal glands to work properly and help your body react to stress.

CORTISOL: Cortisol is a steroid hormone that regulates a wide range of processes throughout the body, including metabolism and the immune response. It also has an especially important role in helping the body respond to stress

Adrenalin: Adrenaline is a hormone released from the adrenal glands and its major action, together with noradrenaline, is to prepare the body for 'fight or flight'.

1.3.2 How stress act on the body

Stress stimulate by nervous pathway Adreno medulla to produce ADRENALIN affecting many organs

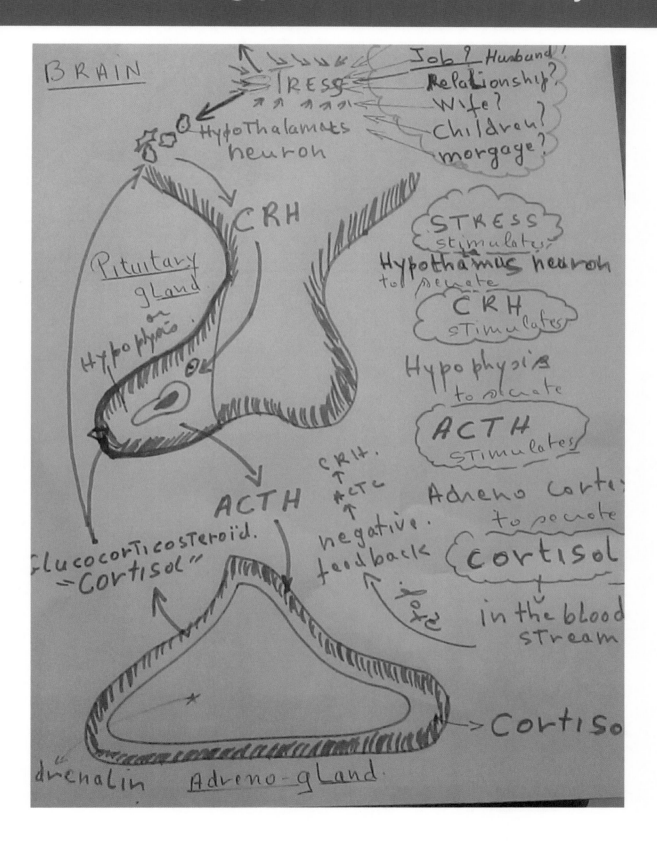

Physical signs Of stress

-Headaches or dizziness

-Muscle tension or pain

-Stomach problems

-Chest pain or a faster heartbeat

-Sexual problems

Mental signs of stress

-Difficulty concentrating

-Struggling to make decisions

- Feeling overwhelmed

-Constantly worrying

-Being forgetful

-Changes in behaviour

-Being irritable and snappy

-Sleeping too much or too little

-Eating too much or too little

-Avoiding certain places or people

-Drinking or smoking

1.3.3 Causes of stress (recap)

our individual genes, upbringing and

experiences

a) difficulties in our personal lives and relationships

b) big or unexpected life changes, like moving to a new house, having

a baby or starting to care for someone

c) money difficulties, like debt or struggling to afford daily

essentials

d) health issues, either for you or someone close to you

e) pregnancy and children

f) problems with housing, like the conditions, maintenance or

tenancy

g) feeling lonely and unsupported

1.3.4 Ten actions steps to take to overcome stress

1. Identify sources of stress

2. Take control

3. Plan ahead

4. Physical activity

5. Challenge yourself

6. look for the positives

7. Reduce alcohol, nicotine & caffeine

8. Break task down into manageable chunks

9. Accept the things you cannot change

10. help other people

Chap 2 : Lifting your spirit up

2.1 Curse or blessing in 2020

In 10 year, times from now, what will you say about year 2020?

Everybody agree that we will draw a line in the sand and say, this was the moment the world has shifted: the traditional economy has adjusted towards the digital economy with lot of businesses closing down , jobs lost drawing uncertainty to the future of working class.

In 2020 our social life has been modified, the prospect for a meaningful and impactful life has changed.

Now question yourself?

Is year 2020 a blessing for you or a curse to you? Answer that question for yourself.

When we look at around us, the change becomes a Must,

what does it mean to us? Of course, It becomes imperative to shift ourselves the way we see things and we act on them, we need the take decisions for this to happen.

The wise man said: Events happening in your life do not control your life, but your decisions do.

Every one of you has a certain belief about how we define ourselves, the story you always tell yourself, that is your identity.

To begin with

The 4 winning punches of healthy life

-Firstly, we will have to throw -away believes that do not serve us or help us.

-Secondly try to change the story we tell ourselves,

If you say "I am a winner", you will find the way to win, if you say "I am a champion", you will find the pathway to become a champion, in whatever you do.

What usually happen to us is the fight between your conscious mind and your subconscious mind.

If you declare; I am a winner through your conscious mind straight away your subconscious mind says the opposite.

What to do in this instance?

Start to train your brain so that what you say is agreed by your subconscious mind.

We do know that the power behind belief in undeniable, your belief can create, your belief can destroy.

A statement of the wise man say this: The strongest force in human personality is the need to stay consistent how we define ourselves.

In other word your "I am" is stronger when associated to any words.

Your identity influences the way we think, what we do, we do not do.

Changing your identity make your behaviour change, your emotion changes permanently.

When we look at into history:

Crisis **causes** people **to create**, **to growth**, to **think differently**, to **solve problems**, **to lead**, that is why 2020 is happening for us and not to us.

We really need now more than ever to adjust our believes, shift our identity by taking massive actions until we reach what we want to reach in life.

Have a look at some of emotions encounter by everyone of us

2.2 Depression and anxiety

I want to briefly contrast that with anxiety, because anxiety and depression are two of the most common emotional states that all of us experience at different points in our lives.

Anxiety is primarily an emotion related to worry and fear about the future. So, it is anticipating apprehension about what might happen in the future. And this includes fear for health and safety. Right now, we are seeing the covid 19 patient.

Some are experiencing apprehension about that,

Other anxiety about being late for you to take an exam or make an appointment or to catch a plane.

Fear of the dark, fear of being alone. These are all worrying about what might happen in the future.

The symptoms include frequent urination, a lump in the throat, but rapid heart rate, rapid heart rate and so on.

Depression

2.2.1.1 Clinical aspects

Depression is another common emotional state that we all experience from time to time. it is related to the past rather than the future. It is related to a loss or suffering a loss. It is already happened and now having to adjust to live in it where we have experienced that loss,

this includes *sadness*, an *empty feeling*, *despair*, *cheerfulness*, *negative thoughts*.

Many people experience fatigue and want to sleep a lot. They may be short tempered. They may experience trouble of appetite.

They might eat more and gain weight or they might lose their appetite, might eat at all; in the more severe forms of depression, there may be *thoughts of death or even suicide.*

According studies in USA it is shown that the frequency of depression in the population is that about eight percent of the adult in US population is diagnosed with a clinical condition called major depression.

2.2.1.2 Categories of depression

We are going to talk about different categories of depression in just a moment. So major depression is where somebody is depressed chronically and may require medication.

This is more common in women than men. 70 percent of women have major depression, 30 percent of males.

The 4 winning punches of healthy life

Sometimes we are not sure if that is because women are more inclined to go to a doctor, whether depressed than males. But we think that women emotionally are more prone to depression for a genetic and hormonal reasons than males.

Depression also becomes more common in the elderly and again, part of that may be anticipation of one is mortality. Confronting mortality, which can be depressing.

Now, there are genetic factors that can affect one is tendency to become depressed. It is been suggested that as much as 40 percent of the individuals with major depression and may be accounted for by genetic factors, there has been research on this. More research is continuing. They there are exist what are known as vulnerability genes and resiliency genes. Vulnerability genes are related to where somebody is genetically, after experiencing a loss, gets emotionally devastated more than others.

Resiliency genes are related to where other people, after they experience a loss. They are depressed, but they bounce back more rapidly. They return to their previous lifestyle more readily; and again, these may be genetic factors.

Also, there is a neurotransmitter, as it is called, the neurotransmitter theory. There are several different neurotransmitters in our brain, and it is believed that imbalances in these neurotransmitter levels may lead to different types of emotional or behavioural states, including depression.

The three major neurotransmitters that you should have some appreciation fo
Serotonin: *seem to affect mood, anxiety, and even obsessive-compulsive disorders. Some medications are designed to elevate or raise the serotonin levels.*

-**Dopamine:** levels seem to affect motivation and pleasure.

Elevated dopamine levels increase motivation and pleasure,

- **Epinephrine neurotransmitter** levels affect your level of alertness and energy levels.

Now there are environmental factors and we mentioned that depression is related to a loss; these are things that happen in one is life. These can include divorce, loss of a job, loss of health where somebody is diagnosed with cancer or diagnosed or just had a heart attack or diagnosed with Parkinson's disease or Alzheimer's disease. These can be devastating when one is diagnosed with these commonly results in depression.

Now, another environmental factor that can lead to depression is gloomy weather in fact, there is a category of depression called sad seasonal affective disorder. We will get to in a moment that is related to too much exposure to gloomy weather. Also, certain medications predispose an individual to becoming depressed.

But the specific medication that we highlighted that we do want you to know where corticosteroids like prednisone; individuals who take corticosteroids for an extended period of time, can affect them emotionally and could include causing or contributing to depression.

Progesterone, which is found in birth control pills, oral contraceptives can lead to emotional effects, including depression.

Now, as we mentioned earlier, there are different types of depression; The most common depression that we all experience in our lives is technically called an adjustment disorder with depressed mood; it really means exactly what it says. This is sadness in response to a real personal loss; the person must adjust, and they will adapt.

The 4 winning punches of healthy life

It will take a while for them to heal from the divorce, a loss of job, a medical diagnosis, financial problems and so on and they will be depressed. But the good news is that most people heal after a few months from this and come out of it adjusted.

Having made the adjustment, chronic depression is clinically called is a major depressive disorder or clinical depression.

This is severe depression that does usually require medication; as we mentioned earlier, about eight percent of the US population is on medication for clinical depression.

The third type of depression is called post-partum depression; about 12 percent of women after childbirth experience severe depression and again, that is usually they heal from that. It is probably related to changes in hormone levels. There may be genetic factors that predispose women to postpartum depression.

We had mentioned previously that gloomy weather can lead to depression. This is known as seasonal affective disorder or sad. We saw about five percent of the US population experiences this. This is common in for example, where 300 days of the year it is gloomy, overcast, and cloudy and rainy; that can be depressing.

2.2.1.3 Dealing with depression

Incidentally, the treatment for that, at least in part, is to get more sunlight. Even artificial light with a spectrum that is more like the sun.

What are the non-pharmacological approaches to depression?

We just mentioned the use of sun light and now let see the

number one, most importantly,

1) Physical activity to cure depression

Why physical exercise has an antidepressant effect; makes us feel better even when we are not in depressed state.

These include the release of endorphins, neurotransmitters, the so-called runner's high.

During exercise, our body temperature rises; that is why even a hot shower or bath may be beneficial.

Why exercise may be beneficial is increased circulation throughout the body, including the brain, a reduction of inflammation. Exercise increases our resilience to physical and emotional stress. Another factor that can be beneficial for one is depressed is eating healthy and reducing one is sugar intake.

2) Psychotherapy to cure depression

psychotherapy or counselling.

3 steps procedure approach
- Change your Mental state first
- Secondly tell the story of people who went the same problem
- Strategies Tactics

Seven Actions steps   to change your State

1. Cold exposure (take a cold bath)

2. Heat exposure (until you sweat)

3. Comedy specials (laughing session)

4. Exercise any sport

5. Breathing method

6. Meditation

7. Keep a journal

8. No caffeine, no alcohol

Breakthrough

-How in your life you can create breakthrough?
In life the way we approach things, our believe about life and the mental game determine our succes or failure; In order to take control of these forces we need to take massive actions to be successful.

The 4 winning punches of healthy life

-We definine breakthrough as "a moment in time where suddenly the impossible becomes possible.
you see your circumstances in a new way and everything changes"
Breakthrough can be create in 3 steps
-Changing your Strategy
-Changing your story
-Changing your state

1 Strategy
What is the right strategy for achieving your goal?
Strategy is a specific way of doing things, a recipe , a formulae, we follow to achieve something.
Strategy can be wrong or right
Strategy can be seasonal meanning that it should be implemented at a specify time in order to give result.

2 Story
What is the limiting story do you need to divorce or let go and what new story you will embrace?
If you say " I have tried everything " that means there is no way out!, is it true or false? because if you try everything at some point the result will come.
Remember "Change your story change your life!"

Anxiety

Somebody has anxiety and they do not even know why; about five percent of the population has anxiety to the point that they are being treated for it. We do know that it is more common in women. This is true with many behavioural and emotional disorders.

The 4 winning punches of healthy life

However, we do not really know whether it is more common in women than men or whether simply women are more likely to go to a doctor. Regarding that, men are more likely to go to the bar. All right, but I suspect that it probably is a bit more complicated for women just physiologically.

Again, anxiety is associated with fears of worry, dread; here is the bottom line out of proportion to the actual likelihood of real problem.

In other words, it is one thing if you have a lot of fear. But if you simply have a lot of fear and anxiety, that is beyond really the probability of something. If somebody is really; has a lot of anxiety about earthquakes. All right, the big one could happen. But on a day to day basis, what is the probability on any given day that we really must worry about earthquakes?

You know, if you are so dumb, if somebody is going around every single day, then that is kind of disproportionate to the real problem.

What are some examples? I mentioned earthquake. The fear for health and safety. There are people or you know, hypochondriacs that are worried about you going to get cancer or whatever it is, anxiety about being late for appointments, cause you are somebody who have no anxiety and or lack of fear of the dark.

How about that one fear of being alone? You know, there is a whole bunch of these.

What are the symptoms of anxiety?

Increase muscle tension commonly must go to the bathroom frequently. Difficulty in swallowing exaggerated startle response. Having trouble sleeping; that is called insomnia and maybe nightmares when one does go to sleep and trembling, sweating, nausea.

We do want to make a distinction between classic anxiety and what is known as performance anxiety. Performance anxiety is also referred to as stage fright. And stage fright is where you are anxious in performing and your heart speeds up and your blood pressure rises and you really get exhibiting as empathic risk, a sympathetic response; your stress; this is really an anxiety performance.

Your stage fright is just classic stress. But that is a little bit different than classic anxiety; in fact, you will notice there was stage fright since it is really related to a sympathetic response; Increased heart rate.

Classic anxiety called stage fright. If we think of an actor who is got to go out on stage, they are understandably anxious and stressed and they have got to go out there and perform well. I think in many ways you have got to go out there and perform.

2.3 Healthy thinking

Do you ever think negatively or worry about things by going over things again and again in your mind, just like other aspects of life? We can all fall into different habits. These sorts of unhelpful habits of thinking or unhelpful thoughts can spoil your life.

Some people may find they dwell on the negative. For instance, I will not enjoy it if I go, while others criticise themselves all the time saying things like I am much better at it than me.

Whereas for some others that at the very worst to happen and jump to the worst conclusion about everything. I always mess things up. Or we may get focus on what other people think about us. Keep worrying that others find us boring or do not like us much at all. They think I am stupid if I say this. While these things might sometimes be true at times when we feel stressed out, although we tend to notice this sort of thoughts far more often, they become harder to put out of mind. And the thing about these sorts of unhelpful thoughts habits is just that unhelpful and usually not true as well.

But when we believe these things they worth and how we feel and also affect what we do.; these sorts of unhelpful thoughts tell us that we are useless or that nobody likes us or not to bother doing things; if we believe them, not on them, they cause us to stop doing things, to withdraw. We end up feeling even worse.

So unhelpful thoughts talk us not going out with friends, applying for that new job. Speaking up at meetings or simply doing something nice for you; of course, the less you do, the worse you feel, the worse you feel, the less you do; we get stuck in a vicious circle.

The 4 winning punches of healthy life

You may have noticed that at times when we feel stressed out the low, that is when these thoughts get supercharged and pop into our minds a lot more if we fill our minds with these sort of thoughts.

We get to feel worse and worse. what the people often tell us when we were; we like that. Try not to think about it. Let us just see if that works right now. And I will do it, too.

As both of us tried hard not to think about a white polar bear. If you are anything like me, you will find you can think of nothing else. But if you did manage it, they must spend a lot of mental energy thinking about perhaps a black polar bear or a car or whatever that is the key lesson.

We need to find a more effective, practical way of dealing with our unhelpful thoughts; doing something about these thoughts can help boost how you feel and help you get going again. Here is a typical example of somebody having unhelpful thoughts.

Parveen is looking for a new job and is working on her CV; she has run out of things to say about herself and the personal statements; she starts a slump in a chair and goes out of the window; Some of the things Parveen are saying to herself are what is the point?

Loads of people will be applying someone else and more experts will probably get the job. I cannot be bothered with this. Will I ever get a job? and as a result, she gives up, never sent in her application. Instead, she goes and sits down feeling upset and useless.

These thoughts are unhelpful because they work and how Parveen feels. Imagine if you were saying these things to yourself over and over, day on day, week on week. Slowly, that is unhelpful.

The 4 winning punches of healthy life

Thoughts would grind you down, just like in Parvin case; Anyone of us would feel angry, upset, frustrated, embarrassed, guilty, sad, lonely, and so on.

let us move on to what to do when this happens.

First, we need a plan and our plans called the amazing bad thought busting programme or a Beattie BP for short.

Firstly, label the thought; For example, you might find yourself taking things to heart, beating yourself up, having a gloomy view of the future, being your own worst critic, jumping to the worst conclusions.

If others see you badly or taking responsibility for everything.

These are patterns we can all fall into time and time again. You may have already noticed that you are more prone to one or more of these thinking styles or that you notice them more than usual when you get upset, when you notice one of these unhelpful thoughts before you start to get too upset and caught up in it.

Just mentally trying to step back and stick a label on it. Oh, that is just one of those bad thoughts; when you label and unhelpful thoughts, this way begins to lose its power. You realise this is just part of being upset.

It is not the truth.

It is just one of those bad thoughts. You could even say to it, your Rumbold are not playing that game again.

Secondly, leave it alone. Now you know what it is. Mentally, turn your back on the bad thought; do not challenge it or try to argue with it.

The 4 winning punches of healthy life

Just let it be.

Break that cycle where the thoughts go round and round in our heads, making us feel worse. Instead, take a step back and let the thought just be instead of getting caught up in it.

Choose to think about what you are doing right now. Really focus on this moment, on the conversation you may be having.

Sometimes people find it helpful. Mentally placing the unhelpful thoughts in the corner of the room like a child has just been told, often must sit in the corner and be quiet. That can take some practise because like celebrities, our thoughts love attention. But it said, just let them be.

No, shut up eventually.

Thirdly, stand up to it; do not be bossed about by bad thoughts, bad thoughts are like bullies. They sound strong, but really, they are weak underneath and they tell lies. They say you will not like doing anything.

They say you will fail if you try to tell your rubbish or you are scared, and nobody likes you. But this is just a bad thought, not the truth. So, do not be bullied. If the thought says do not do it, the thought says, cannot, they hand right back at it? Call his bluff and see what really happens.

Stand up to that bully and you will find that what they are seeing just is not true.

Fourthly, give yourself a break, but also how we beat ourselves up when we are upset. They make us say things to ourselves that we would never say to a friend. So if you are having trouble with a bad thought, think, well, the person you love most in the whole world would say to you right now, they disagree with the bad thoughts, would not they?

The 4 winning punches of healthy life

They would remind you that you are not rubbish or stupid or bound to fail to try this, go into a room by yourself and say what your friend would say to you out loud. Say it again in a kind voice and remember that bad thoughts tell lies. People who love you tell you the truth.

Trust these positive thoughts and let them help you get rid of the bad thoughts.

Firstly, look at the situation differently. First, imagine what it would be like if it were a friend, not you, who was experiencing the unhelpful.

What advice would you give now, give the same advice to yourself?

Also, put your thought or worry into perspective. Will it matter so much in six months' time?

Will you remember what the problem was? If it will matter in six months, it is probably not that important now. Also, how would others deal with the problem? Think about someone who seems to handle problems well and work out what they do, how they think in that situation.

2.4 Fear

Psychologists believe that one of the strategies to tackle fear is focus. These are the 3 ways of focusing

Where are you focusing?

First focal point

Are you focusing on what you have or on what is missing in your life, most people in this life are focusing on what is missing, we have heard words like: I do not have money, I do not have time, I am not comfortable… the truth is, when you are focusing on what is missing, it drives you into more depressions than ever, more stresses.

However when you are focussing on what you have, like having a good health, having a family, having friends, a country, you become more energised and you will be thankful of all those gifts that empower you with more strength and the opportunity to say thank you in your life to your creator.

Second focal point

Are you focusing on what you can control or what you cannot control?

Focusing on what you can control like your skills, your inner courage, push you to go forwards, to be creative…

The 4 winning punches of healthy life

Unlike when you focus on what you can not control like the Covid-19 itself, you become worries, stressed at least be focus on your immune system that you can control by applying concepts laid out in this eBook.

Third focal point

Are you focusing on the past, the present, or the future?

Most people look at in the past, the present and the future.

If you spent more time in the future, it becomes incredibly stressful for you.

If you live in the present, it gives you confidence, you can control what is surrounding you.

The better would be:

If spend much time in the past you become non performant.

living in the present with your feet on the ground by being determined, creative and passionate about what you are doing to make your goals successful in the future, using the tools you have learned in the past.

Chap 3: Dietary intake

3.1 Balanced diet

No one can deny the need of a balanced diet in maintaining our body and mind healthier.

We do need

a. Proteins

b. Carbohydrate

c. Fat

d. Water

e. Vitamins & Mineral

The 4 winning punches of healthy life

The Covid-19 outbreak has highlighted the importance of one nutrient the body do required to fight infection and

The 4 winning punches of healthy life

3.1.1 Vitamin D.

In this talk, we are examining, one aspect of metabolic disease, which is the lack of one crucial nutrient in the Body.

Before we go into the link between Vit D deficiency and viral infection, let have a look at the basic about this important chemical Vit D.

This nutrient is a vitamin and hormone at the same time, it controls the expression of thousands of genes, in others word, thousands of physiological processes depend on this nutrient inside the body.

This unusual chemical is got from the UVB exposure and those who live in northern hemisphere will be getting more as we are heading to summer' months between March and end of September.

3.1.2 Sources of Vit D

- UVB exposure
- Fish such as Salmon, Catfish, mackerel, Bluefish, Herring.
- Mushroom

What our body used Vit D for?

Vit D play a role in

- Musculo- skeleton health, where Vit D is required in bone formation to

incorporate calcium in it.

-In diabetes, the pancreas cell involved in producing insulin required Vit D to work

3.1.3 How long should be exposed to sunshine?

Studies suggest that

20 minutes of exposure is required

-10% of the body, neck, face, arms…)

How deficiency in Vit D is expressed?

In the UK, the optimum level of Vit D, the guidance shows this level is

- 25 nanogram/ml of serum, under that level, you are declared deficient

In the USA, this optimum is about

-30 nanogram/ml of serum

Vitamin D

Studies in America shows that 30 % of the black African American

population are deficient in this chemical.

Black and Asian population are struggling to reach this optimum of 25

or 30 in normal summer months, this should be adjusted by vitamin

supplementation.

-The melanin, which is the pigment find in dark skin act as a Sun cream preventing more absorption of radiation in the skin.

Some studies also suggest that low level of Vit D expose the body to some types of cancer.

It appears as well that **people who are obese, with higher body Index, have low level of Vit D,** Studies explained that the Vit D is a liposoluble vitamin, meaning that it is stored in the fat cell and made inactive and unavailable in the bloodstream.

Vit D has variety of sources: Meat, Eggs, peaches, Fish, Papaya, Squash, Melon, Avocado, carrots.

According to a recent study:

Anthony Fauci, Director of the National Institute of Allergy, and Infectious Diseases, advising the US government said:

The most "so: -called immune boosting supplements" actually do "nothing." However, there are two vitamins Fauci does recommend helping keep your immune system healthy.

"If you are deficient in vitamin D, that does have an impact on your susceptibility to infection. So, I would not mind recommending, and I do it myself taking vitamin D supplements," Fauci, 79, said during an Instagram Live on TV, when asked about immune-boosting supplements.

(In fact, researchers at the University of Chicago Medicine recently found a link between vitamin D deficiency and the likelihood of being infected with Covid-19 — those with an untreated deficiency were more likely to test positive.

The 4 winning punches of healthy life

Vitamin D is important to the function of the immune system and vitamin D supplements have previously been shown to lower the risk of viral respiratory tract infections," David Meltzer, chief of hospital medicine at UChicago Medicine and lead author of the study said in a press release;

In addition to vitamin D,

DR Fauci said that vitamin C is "a good antioxidant." "So, if people want to take a gram or two at the most [of] vitamin C, that would be fine," he said.

3.1.2 Vitamin C

"contributes to immune defence by supporting various cellular functions" of the body's immune systems, according to 2017 study published by The National Institutes of Health, and vitamin C also appears to prevent and treat "respiratory and systemic infections." according to researchers.)

But "any of the other concoctions and herbs I would not do," Fauci said.

During another interview Fauci said in clinical studies most "so-called" immune-boosting supplements did not really help people unless they had some sort of a deficiency.

If fact, a lot of these herbs "either do nothing, or, if you take too much of them, they harm you," Fauci said.

The 4 winning punches of healthy life

Overall, the best way to boost your immune system is to get good sleep and exercise, Fauci said. "Those are the things that are so much better than a bunch of herbs that really have never really been shown to do that,

and Fauci said in the July issue of InStyle Magazine that he also made time to power walk at least 3.5 miles a day to relieve stress and maintain good health during the pandemic. Fauci, who has been director of the National Institute of Allergy and Infectious Diseases since 1984, used to run up to seven miles a day at lunchtime, but switched to power walking because it is gentler on his body.

Chap 4 : Sleep pattern

4.1 Sleeping

In this part of our talk we will focus on sleep pattern to help yourself to some common life difficulties. In this session, we are focussing on how to sleep better.

Sleep is crucial to all of us. We need this to feel well physically as well as to boost how we feel emotionally. We can all identify with not sleeping properly for a night or two when perhaps something exciting, like a birthday or a holiday is about to occur, or for something we are worried or concerned about, like an interview or a family crisis.

And not sleeping properly is a bad start to any day. But if it just lasts for a day or two, most people could put up with it. But it is when we cannot sleep properly for several days or weeks that it gets harder and harder to cope.

This session will help build your understanding of ways to get a restful night's sleep. I will point out some easy and practical things that can help. Here is a typical example of someone who is not been sleeping well for several weeks.

Simon is studying for exams and has been spending a lot of time in his bedroom working hard. He has also been using energy drinks, coffee to keep focus as he works. And this is helping him up so much that although he is feeling exhausted when he gets into bed, he finds his not able to fall asleep. He ends up tossing and turning in bed, watching the clock, and then finds it difficult getting up in the morning because he feels so tired. Do you ever feel like this? The good news is that there are lots of things you can do that may help you sleep better.

The 4 winning punches of healthy life

A matter of breaking things down and making small changes that will add up.

First, you need to plan how you go to sleep, get into a sleep routine, go to bed and get up at the same time every day and don't lay in on nap when you should be awake as this upsets your body clock and makes it harder to drop off. Also, be good to yourself and gently whine down for half an hour before bed.

If you have a warm bath with bubbles or salts or soap and nice warm milk, drink and listen to them. Soothing music. If you find that reading relaxes you, read a happy book, but maybe not a thriller.

Make sure your bedroom is warm and cosy and dark. If the Bed is chilli had a blanket or another duvet and go back to the hot water bottle, you used love as a kid. If it is just too hot. Use a fan or get one of those cherry stone pillows.

You can cool down in the freezer and open the window, drop the duvet and sleep under a sheet. Is the bat itself really comfy, if not change your pillows? Or try turning the mattress or maybe the curtains were a bit. In which case, try thicker ones or blackout linings. Perhaps things were a bit noisy outside. Maybe get some earplugs.

Some people find that alcohol seems to make them feel sleepy, but do remember, it is just a shallow sleep that does not last for long.

And you will probably find you have to get up in the middle of the night to go to the loo. So, try not to drink alcohol in the hour or so before bed.

Exercise is also a bad idea. Just before bed, although getting physically tired might seem OK. She is not as good as slowly winding down. So again, try not to do anything strenuous near bedtime.

The 4 winning punches of healthy life

Do not smoke either, because smoking wakes you up. So, if you do smoke every cigarette, at least half an hour or so before your bath.

Watching TV in bed is also a no, plus watch it come down a little bit before your bath. But try and get rid of the television in your bedroom and think about losing the radio, too. Or at least do not listen to it just before sleeping or in the middle of the night and take those books downstairs, because reading in bed is also against the rules, as is eating.

I hope you are getting the idea that there are only two things allowed in bed, sleep, and sex. Now you have a nice, warm, comfy bedroom. You might just do a little bit more of both. But at first, even after winding down with your warm bath and warm milk drink, you may still be turning things over again and again in your mind.

So here is what to do. Keep a pen and paper by the side of the bed if you have worries going round and round. And he had to keeping you awake. Sit up. Turn on the light. Or instead leave the room if you have a partner and get that piece of paper, cut it into strips and write down one thing that is worrying you.

On each strip and just doing this, separating out each of the things you are worrying about will help you untangle them and make them easier to cope with.

Next, give each worry a day and a time from tomorrow morning onwards when you are going to sit down and really work on sorting it out. So, your first trip might say, I think Mary is upset with me. I will think about three or three o'clock on Thursday.

Perhaps the second might be I do not feel as if I am appreciated at work. I am going to tackle that at six o'clock on Wednesday evening. Try and do this for all the worries left over.

The 4 winning punches of healthy life

Do you have a number of slips with thoughts and days and times on them and look at the slips and promise yourself that you are going to think about each problem on the day you've written them down, but not until then. They will put the slip somewhere where you will not lose them and go back to bed.

You have nothing on your worries schedule now, so you are officially entitled to get some rest. And if you have tried all these different things and still are not sleeping, then get up. And I know it sounds crazy, doesn't it? But get up and go downstairs and sit in a comfy chair and read a book or watch telly or listen to some music and do this until you feel sleepy, tired, then go back to bed if you choose to do this.

Each time we have been in bed away from more than, say, 20 minutes, you will quite quickly break the cycle of lying there and getting upset as he watched the minutes tick by all night. You have made a great start here by completing this session.

But please remember that if these simple tips do not help and if a lack of sleep is affecting your daily life, then it might be time to talk to your practitioner.

4. Physical Activities

Scientific finding suggested that physical exercises is the better way to improve your mental and physical health. It is known to boost your mood and energy levels.

Physical activity can also provide routine and structure your day.

Gymnastic activities are the nicer and easy way to exercise.

There are many exercises plan outside to choose from depend on your lifestyle

- Gymnastic
- Practice 30 min walk a day keeps you healthy
- Practice what it is called The Nordic walking at least once a month it is 1 or two hours walk with sticks.

Nordic Walking

Gymnastic

Need and Requirement

Work out plan

6 min: warming up and stretching properly

The 4 winning punches of healthy life

10 min: Exercises your heart and Lung with cardio work

Out (skipping rope)

10 min: Toning work out and trump up your bum, legs,

arms

10 min: Tone up, Firm up burn fat, work out for legs,

10 min: Tone your tummy

5 min: Cool down routine

Resources:

Professor Cary Cooper, an occupational health expert at the University of Lancaster United Kingdom.

says:

"the keys to good stress management are building emotional strength, being in control of your situation, having a good social network and adopting a positive outlook".

- National Health Service provide this: free psychological therapies like cognitive behavioural therapy (CBT) on the NHS.
- The British Association for Behavioural & Cognitive Psychotherapies (BABCP) keeps a register of all accredited therapists in the UK and The British Psychological Society (BPS) has a directory of chartered psychologists, some of whom specialise in CBT.
- Prof Anna Whittaker (Psychologist and prof of behaviour medicine).(AW)
- Book: Ten Times happier by Owen O'kane.
- Book: Stress proof by Mithu Storoni.
- Book: Peace with God, By Billy Graham
- Website: https://www.nhs.uk/oneyou/ever...
- Dr John Demartini: principles of life and health.
- Dr Joseph Murphy: The power of your subconscious Mind
- Tony Robbins: "Unleash your inner Power" (TR)
- Dr David Yonggi Cho: The 4TH Dimension
- Desmond Tutu and Dalai lama: The book of Joy
- Desmond Tutu: The book of forgiveness
- Dr Joseph Murphy: Magic of Faith
- Prof Steve Fink expert in Biology science at west Los Angeles College USA. (PSF)

Religious groups: Bible (Christianity), Tipitaka (Buddhism), The Vedas and the Upanishads (Hinduism), The Quran and The Hadiths (Islam), The Tanakh and Talmud (Judaism) Guru Granth Sahib (Sikhism) ...

The 4 winning punches of healthy life

Patrice Mbowa Kasongo